IS CHURCH MEMBERSHIP
BIBLICAL?

✕ CULTIVATING BIBLICAL GODLINESS

Series Editors

Joel R. Beeke and Ryan M. McGraw

Dr. D. Martyn Lloyd-Jones once said that what the church needs to do most of all is "to begin herself to live the Christian life. If she did that, men and women would be crowding into our buildings. They would say, 'What is the secret of this?'" As Christians, one of our greatest needs is for the Spirit of God to cultivate biblical godliness in us in order to put the beauty of Christ on display through us, all to the glory of the triune God. With this goal in mind, this series of booklets treats matters vital to Christian experience at a basic level. Each booklet addresses a specific question in order to inform the mind, warm the affections, and transform the whole person by the Spirit's grace, so that the church may adorn the doctrine of God our Savior in all things.

IS CHURCH MEMBERSHIP
BIBLICAL?

RYAN M. MCGRAW
AND RYAN SPECK

REFORMATION HERITAGE BOOKS
GRAND RAPIDS, MICHIGAN

Reformation Heritage Books
3070 29th St. SE
Grand Rapids, MI 49512
616-977-0889
orders@heritagebooks.org
www.heritagebooks.org

Printed in the United States of America
22 23 24 25 26/10 9 8 7 6 5 4 3 2

ISBN 978-1-60178-429-2

For additional Reformed literature, request a free book list from Reformation Heritage Books at the above regular or e-mail address.

IS CHURCH MEMBERSHIP
BIBLICAL?

———✖———

How many membership cards are you currently carrying? Do you have a library membership, a grocery store preferred-customer card, a gym membership, and perhaps others? Most organizations require membership and keep track of their members. We have so many memberships that we can become weary of them. This weariness leads some people to groan when the church, which is a spiritual institution, requires official membership. Thus, it is increasingly common for Christians to question whether church membership is a biblical practice.

As Bereans, Christians are right to ask if church membership is biblical, especially since no one can cite chapter and verse to prove a multistep process for joining the church and being counted on her rolls. If you seek an explicit command in the Bible that insists your name must be included on the membership rolls of a particular church, you will seek in vain. So, then, why do some churches insist on an official process to join their membership while others

do not? The biblical answer to this question will
not be direct, but indirect. Just as a canvas provides
a necessary backdrop to a work of art, so the Bible
assumes the necessity of formal church membership
in order to fulfill the commands and to apply the
promises of Scripture with regard to the church.

We define formal church membership as *a covenant made by a public vow in which a person commits
himself or herself to a local body of believers under the
authority of a well-defined group of church leaders.* This
results in an official record of members who belong
to a local church. We will demonstrate the require-
ment for formal church membership by proving
from Scripture that the church is a visible community, that every Christian must be a member of this
community, and that such membership necessitates
vows and rolls. Then we will conclude by answering
three common objections against formal membership as we have defined it.

THE FOUNDATIONS OF CHURCH MEMBERSHIP:
THE CHURCH AS A COMMUNITY

The Analogy of Citizenship

Throughout Scripture, God describes His people
as a city or a nation: a gathered, defined group of
people living together (e.g., Psalms 46, 48, 87; Matt.
21:43; Phil. 3:20; Heb. 12:22–24; Revelation 21). He
depicts heaven as the city of God (Rev. 21:2) and
Christians as citizens of a heavenly city (Phil. 3:20;
Heb. 11:10). While foreigners may reside in a city or

nation, citizens alone constitute its true membership. They have birth certificates, pay taxes, and obtain passports and other licenses. In other words, they have recognized privileges and responsibilities that noncitizens do not and should not have. The nature of any society, by definition, includes official citizens belonging to it by open and clear documentation and record. Thus, for example, when someone is caught in a criminal act, one of the first points in processing his case is to determine whether or not he is a citizen of that society. In the United States, if he is a citizen, he must be read his rights and treated with a measure of respect and dignity. If he is not a citizen, then the laws of his own country may affect his treatment.

Official status as a citizen and the rights and privileges that attend this status are not peculiar to any one country or time. This principle was true in biblical times as well. The apostle Paul, for example, appealed to his Roman citizenship for similar rights and privileges (e.g., Acts 22:29). When Paul referred to citizenship in the kingdom of God, he understood citizenship much as we do today. Being a citizen entails having official, publicly recognized membership in a community. To be a citizen of a country is to be an official member of its society, a subject of its laws, and a beneficiary of its government. As citizens of the kingdom of God, Christians enjoy all the rights and privileges of living under Christ's rule and government.

Christ has recorded the names of His citizens in His book (Rev. 13:8; 21:27). As it is in every other respect, the church militant (on earth) is a dim reflection of the church triumphant (in glory). When God in His Word uses this language of citizenship to describe our status in the courts of heaven, do you imagine that an official, public commitment to the church on earth would be out of place? Do you believe God forbids on earth the record-keeping His own Son practices in heaven? The church is both visible and invisible. In its visible aspect, we identify the members of the church through their profession of faith in Christ and obedience to Him. In this booklet, we are primarily dealing with membership in this ideal sense—that is, of true believers rather than those who make nominal professions only—since those who make true confessions of faith compose the church's essence. In its invisible character, God alone knows who His elect are and who are truly born of the Spirit. Yet the visible church is made in the image of the invisible church and, as such, reflects its character. Would it not be fitting for those who belong to this invisible society to express their citizenship by belonging to the visible church, which is the earthly expression of this heavenly kingdom? Do you imagine that God would reject official record-keeping on earth while His Son keeps such a record in heaven?

Yet some might maintain that while Jesus keeps His record rightly in the heavenly sphere, citizenship on earth in the hands of men is a cold and lifeless concept. Is belonging to the kingdom of God merely a matter of having the right papers on earth as determined by mere men? In placing church membership in opposition to the nature of a warm, loving society, Christians can, however, unintentionally neglect the full teaching of God's Word. In Scripture, official, public, formal vows are not at variance with living, warm, organic fellowship with other believers and with true, heartfelt, spontaneous devotion to God. For example, consider the analogy of the family.

The Analogy of a Family

Membership in an earthly family is analogous to membership in the church. The Scripture describes God's people, the church, as a family (e.g., Luke 8:21; Gal. 3:26; Eph. 5:25–33; Heb. 2:11; 1 John 3:1–3). Though families can be less loving and cohesive than they ought to be, they are definite units of people living together in close relations. These relations should, and often do, produce warm relationships, which is God's intention (Gen. 2:24; Matt. 19:5; Eph. 5:31). Such love is also Christ's intention for His church. It is the love He has shown to the church (Eph. 5:25), and it is the love He intends for us to show to one another (1 John 4:11).

This description of the church as the family of God helps us to understand (by analogy) what our personal conduct ought to be, both in the family and in the church. The husband should love his wife and give himself for her (Eph. 5:25), just as Christ did for the church. Wives must submit to their husbands and respect them (Eph. 5:22, 33), just as the church loves and respects Christ. Children are obligated to obey their parents in the Lord (Eph. 6:1). Fathers must beware of provoking their children to wrath (Eph. 6:4). They do so by reflecting the just and wise government of the Lord as they, along with their wives, rear their children in the nurture and admonition of the Lord (Eph. 6:4).

While belonging to a family is part of a natural process, it is also an official legal matter. While it is popular for people to speak of starting a family when couples have children, according to Scripture, a family begins with and is constituted by a marriage covenant (Gen. 2:24; Mal. 2:14). The intimacy and unity that should exist between members of a family begin with a husband and wife joined together by covenant in the sight of God through vows. The marriage covenant is a legal covenant, involving officially recorded and publicly taken vows (Ruth 4:10–11; Mal. 2:14; Matt. 22:1–15; Rev. 19:9). This is true in civil society as well as in Scripture. Contractual agreements mean nothing legally unless they are established as a matter of public record with witnesses (Deut. 19:15; Matt. 18:16). For this reason also, the Scripture repeatedly affirms that a marriage can be dissolved only through a certificate of divorce (Deut. 24:1, 3; Isa. 50:1; Mark 10:4). The commitment a man and woman make to each other excludes all other people from the rights, privileges, and duties of that marriage. All others should know that these two people belong to one another; they are off limits to all outsiders. This is why we wear wedding rings—they commemorate publicly our marriage vows.

When we come to Christ, we become part of His church, which is His bride. Because we are born again by the Spirit's power, we are children of God and belong to His family. We belong to the family of God through marriage to Christ. Moreover, much like our public commitments in marriage, He commands us to confess Him before men (Matt. 10:32–33; Luke 12:8–9; Rom. 10:9–10). Do a public vow and an official record make marriage a dry, cold, dusty relationship? On the contrary, publicly and officially declaring their love for and commitment to one another should deepen a couple's love. A couple with no public commitment to one another always has an uncertain and undefined relationship. They have no clearly defined privileges and no binding responsibilities to one another. This is often why men who will not commit to a woman in marriage often speak of not wanting to be tied down and why the women who are with them are often insecure. We could make a similar argument in relation to having children (who then receive birth certificates) and adopting children (another prominent theme in the Scripture to describe God's people). Such official commitments do not in any way contradict the free, vibrant, organic nature of Christianity. Rather, they are part and parcel with it throughout the Bible. We

are related to the triune God and to one another, and
we must dwell together as an official, public covenantal and loving family.

The Analogy of a Body

Even though the church as the family of God provides an intimate portrait of God's relation to His
people, the biblical imagery of the church as the body
of Christ deepens this intimacy. What could more
vividly or clearly demonstrate that God's people are
(and must be) a close, intimate community than the
image of the body? The apostle Paul uses this picture
powerfully in 1 Corinthians 12. Though the body is
composed of many members, it is one organically
unified corpus. While we can distinguish the parts
of the body from the whole, we cannot separate the
parts of the body from the whole. If a member is cut
off, then that member dies. The church, as the body
of Christ, makes sense only if God's people are to
be united in a vibrant, intimately connected whole,
which flows from a vital union with Christ. In Scripture, there is no such thing as a solitary Christian.
If a professing Christian decides to forsake the body
of Christ, then Paul would say that Christian dies.
That person cannot live apart from Christ as the
Head and believers as fellow members of the same
body. Although some professing Christians argue
they can remain apart from the church while united
to Christ, can you imagine an individual part of the
body attached to the head, without the rest of the

body? How grotesque a picture of Christianity that is! It does not fit with the picture of the church as the body of Christ.

Furthermore, many professing Christians, in their disdain for what they call organized religion (ordinarily meaning an official body of professing Christians gathering together in a church as an institution), betray their belief in a false dualism — separating and holding in contradiction the spiritual and the physical aspects of the church. In effect, they believe that the church is spiritually alive and vibrant like a spirit, but they deny that she is also tangibly organized like a body. They attempt to treat the church as something intangible and imperceptible to the human eye. They virtually transform the church into an invisible spirit without a visible body in which to live and to express its life.

In theological terms, such people claim that they are members of the church invisible, but they deny or neglect the importance of the church visible.[1] It is

---

1. The Westminster Confession of Faith 25.1–2 defines invisible and visible church as follows:

The catholic or universal Church, which is invisible, consists of the whole number of the elect, that have been, are, or shall be gathered into one, under Christ the Head thereof; and is the spouse, the body, the fulness of Him that filleth all in all. The visible Church, which is also catholic or universal under the Gospel (not confined to one nation, as before under the law), consists of all those throughout the world that profess the true religion; and of their children: and is the kingdom of the Lord

important to remember that the invisible and visible church terminology does not describe two distinct churches. These terms are two ways of describing aspects of the same church. If you are a living member of Christ's body through faith, then the only way for you to demonstrate this relation is through the visible expression of this body. You can do this only through the church as an institution. As man is made in the image of God and reflects His glory, so the visible church is made in the image of the invisible church and reflects its corporate identity. The Bible never commends or looks favorably upon an isolated, autonomous Christian. There is no such thing as a maverick Christian in the Scripture. Such a concept is diametrically opposed to the nature of the church as community, which is set forth with abundant clarity throughout the Scripture. We challenge anyone to show us a case of an independent Christian living so by divine design (outside of extreme necessity or extraordinary circumstances). A solitary Christian is a sad example of the poor estate of biblical religion in our time. Such people ordinarily display personal rebellion against God's commandments in relation to the Christian life as part of the body of Christ, the fellowship of believers.

Jesus Christ, the house and family of God, out of which there is no ordinary possibility of salvation.

A Practical Observation

These biblical concepts apply to the "church hopper" in our day: the person who jumps from church to church, never settling into any one. Whenever something happens that irritates him in the least, he jumps to another church. Does this reflect that same attitude to the church that the triune God places upon it? How can such a person be vitally connected to God's people in any meaningful sense of the term? As death is separation of the spirit from the body, so those who claim to have the spirit of Christianity without expressing spiritual vitality in the body of the church appear spiritually dead instead of alive, whatever they may claim. To put it as James does with regard to the claim of faith, what good is it to *say* you are a citizen of God's kingdom if your works do not evidence living in this community (James 2:14, 26)? The members of the invisible church express their life through commitment to the visible church. How can they do otherwise? Have you ever experienced a time when you were, practically speaking, cut off from weekly and intimate fellowship with other believers? Perhaps you traveled to a foreign country for a time. Perhaps you moved to an area without a church nearby. If so, then was this not a difficult, waning time in your spiritual life? Did you not miss the sweet fellowship and mutual love and concern that you knew with your brethren in the church as a society, family, and body? Surely such times drive the value of committed fellowship and true community home to our hearts. God established the community of believers for our good. It is necessary for our spiritual growth in the grace and knowledge of Christ.

This description of the church as a divinely ordained community does not prove the case for formal church membership, but it is the necessary backdrop for it, for defective views of church membership often reflect defective views of the church itself.

THE DUTY OF CHURCH MEMBERSHIP: WE MUST JOIN THIS COMMUNITY

The biblical description of the church as a community implicitly requires us to join this community. This is the case for at least two reasons. Both of these reasons highlight the truth that, ordinarily, it is neither desirable nor possible to live the Christian life alone.

The Interdependence of Believers

The community of the church is so vitally important simply because we need each other. The apostle Paul drives this point home in 1 Corinthians 12:21. The eye cannot say to the hand that it does not need it. The head cannot say to the feet that it does not require them. It would be absurd to treat our physical bodies in this way. Yet Paul indicates that this is precisely how Christians often treat the church. Rather, as with the members of the body, so with the church there must be interdependence between Christians, not independence of Christians from one another. For we are differing members of the same body.

It is true that all genuinely saved church members have the fruit of the Spirit (Gal. 5:22–26) in greater or lesser measure. Yet the Spirit has also especially gifted us in various ways in order to complement each other's faith and service through exercising these gifts. Some of us are called to be teachers and preachers. Some of us are especially equipped to administrate. Some are gifted for mercy ministries above others. Some have a remarkable ability to encourage others. Why has Christ distributed such gifts among His people? It is for the edifying of His body (Eph. 4:7–16). Our fellowship with one another is necessary in order to live the Christian life and to express the life of Christ's body.

No one can live well alone. People made in the image of the triune God need fellowship. God needs no one. The communion of the Father, the Son, and the Holy Spirit is a fellowship that accepts no supplement and requires no complement. Yet man is needy. He needs God. The God whom he needs and reflects is a being in communion. Part of man's renewal in God's image (2 Cor. 5:17) consists in his communion with God and with God's church. The Christian is created for Christian fellowship with God and with those who are in fellowship with God.

The Mutual Responsibilities of Believers

Believers not only need one another; they also have duties to perform toward one another. The necessity of Christian fellowship and the responsibilities resulting from that fellowship are joined inseparably by God; let no man rend them asunder. If God created us to be a body of believers needing fellowship, and if He equipped us to help one another in the faith, then we must exercise our gifts for the blessing of fellow believers, and not for our own private benefit. God commands not to withhold from one another what the other needs. When you read Scripture, you find multiple "one another" commands. Wayne Mack notes fifty-eight such commands.[2] He writes,

> All these commands are written in the present tense. This means we're to be constantly doing these things. The lives of every believer should be characterized by the fulfillment of these commands toward other believers. We're to be constantly devoted to one another, praying for one another, honoring one another, greeting one another, and motivating one another to love and good works. If this is true, then it also follows that we must be physically present with other people in order to do these things.... We cannot possibly fulfill these kinds of commands to every person in the world. We do not have the time or the

---

2. Wayne Mack, *To Be or Not to Be a Church Member, That Is the Question* (Merrick, N.Y.: Calvary Press Publishing, 2004), 26. Consider, e.g., the following: Romans 12:16; Galatians 6:1–2; 1 Corinthians 12:25–26; Hebrews 3:13; 10:24; Colossians 3:16; and James 5:16.

resources to do it, no matter how much we would like to. We have to be selective about the people with whom we're going to work in fulfilling these commands.[3]

In other words, we clearly have the responsibility to love one another, but we have limited resources to do so as individuals. Therefore, we must focus our attention upon a local body of believers. While some would agree with this need to focus our attention upon one fellowship, they insist that we can keep these "one another" commands without formal church membership: "Can't we be a community without belonging officially to a church? Can't we fulfill these commands and needs outside of the church as an institution through parachurch organizations?" Therefore, many professing believers have no official relation to any church, but they regularly attend or even minister in churches or in informal Christian groups. Some churches even forbid (or don't offer) both membership and ordination. Do such people lack the intimate and loving experience of the church as outlined above? Are they really defective in fulfilling Christ's commands to the church through His apostles?

---

3. Mack, *To Be or Not to Be a Church Member*, 29.

THE FORM AND MEANS OF CHURCH MEMBERSHIP: MEMBERSHIP ROLLS AND MEMBERSHIP VOWS

At least four practical reasons solidify the need for membership rolls and formal membership vows: the relationship between church members and church officers, God's covenantal dealings with mankind, the process of church discipline, and the right of the congregation to elect her own officers. The material above shows the need for formal church membership in terms of the nature of the church and the duty to join her. The material below shows the form that such membership should take.

The Relationship between Church Members and Church Officers

The relationship and responsibilities between church members and church officers necessitate formal church membership. From the beginning, God instituted various means of governance for His people. He made Adam Eve's head before the fall (1 Tim. 2:11–13). Thus, God provided human leadership even in a perfect world with perfect people. A necessary implication of such perfect governance is that human governance is not a necessary evil; it is a necessary good. Even in a sin-cursed world, human governance continues to be a necessary good as supplied by God for the blessing of His people. Our Lord called Abraham to be the head of his household, which constituted the people of God at that time (Gen. 18:19). God provided priests, prophets, and kings to be over His people (Leviticus 9; 1 Sam. 3:20; 16:13; 1 Chron. 23:13; Amos 2:11). He called apostles to lead the church under the New Testament (Matt. 10:1–8; Acts 1:24–25; Eph. 2:20; 3:5; 4:11). He set forth the eldership as a perpetual office in the church (1 Tim. 3:1–7; 5:17; Titus 1:5–9). God has always made it clear that for the good of men He intends for them to be ruled by other men according to the authority structures of His choosing and of His designation. In fact, Jesus gave church leaders as one of the gifts He purchased by His own blood for the good of His church (Eph. 4:8, 11–16). The church is the authority structure under which God has placed all Christians for their blessing. Sometimes it is difficult to see how such men are a blessing for Christ's church. Most church leaders themselves are bewildered at times as to why God called them and how He could use them. Nonetheless, to the glory of His grace alone, He uses men of clay feet to bless His people in various ways.

However we understand the exact form of church government, we should at least be able to affirm that the church is a body of professing members under divinely sanctioned officers. For example, Acts 15 describes what is known as the Jerusalem Council. A troublesome teaching arose among God's people regarding circumcision and importing Jewish rites into the Gentile church. In response, the apostles and elders gathered in Jerusalem to address the problem through the use of Scripture, debate, and prayer. The delegates sent to this council reflected the authority structure that God had appointed in the church through His Word. They were not leaders of parachurch organizations. They were extraordinary (apostles) and ordinary (elders) church officers. The elders were the elected leaders of local churches who led the people and under whose authority the people submitted themselves.[4] The council arrived at its decision by appealing to Scripture rather than to apostolic authority (Acts 15:16–17), even though the apostles were present. The decision was nonetheless ascribed to the Holy Spirit (Acts 15:28). The apostles and elders sent this decision to local churches in many regions with the expectation that all should follow their directions (Acts 16:4).

Hebrews 13:17 further highlights the mutual responsibilities that God enjoins both on the officers and on the members of the church. The writer of Hebrews commands his audience to submit to those who rule over them on the grounds that such rulers must give an account for their souls. In His Word, God assumes that there will be shepherds over His people. He holds those shepherds accountable for how they rule His sheep. How can they be responsible for a definite body of Christians if they

---

4. For example, in Acts 14:23, the Greek verb used to describe the process of choosing elders is *cheirotonéō*, which lexicons universally recognize to mean "choose or elect, likely by raising the hand."

cannot define the bounds of that body? Are they accountable for those souls who come and go as they please? Can such people obey the command of the text when they have no commitment to the local body or to its officers? How can they fulfill these mutual responsibilities without formal commitments from both parties (vows) and membership rolls of some kind? The Word of God does not denigrate authority. Men may abuse the power of church government through their sin, but this does not mean that the government Christ instituted in His church is sinful. This passage commands us to embrace this authority structure as part of our duty and love to God. Certainly, when forced to choose between the two, we must obey God and not men (e.g., Acts 5:29). We must submit to our elders only insofar as they minister according to God's Word. Nonetheless, elders remain God's authority structure for His church today. Our Lord Jesus Christ instituted local authorities to rule over His bride. These governing authorities exercise spiritual power only. Church power is ministerial and declarative, not magisterial and legislative. Church power is not carnal or coercive; it is not by the sword. However, this does not mean that church officers do not exercise genuine authority under Christ their Head.

If God has given an official authority structure to govern His church, then why do many Christians today believe that they can fulfill their responsibility to the church with no tangible commitment to a local church and to her officers? Could it be, at least for some, that the objection is really against the divine mandate to submit to church authority? Could it be that the spirit of radical individualism that pervades our culture has jaded our view of church membership? How do you respond to the language of Hebrews 13:17—"obey" and "submit" to those (a plurality of rulers, not simply to Jesus in the singular) who "rule over you"? How can you apply this without membership?

It is no surprise, therefore, that the apostle Paul taught Titus the need for a plurality of elders in every local church (Titus 1:5; cf. Acts 14:23). The language of *overseer*, *ruler*, and *shepherd* necessitates ruling over a particular body of believers. Thus, elders especially govern local congregations. For example, in Acts 20:17 Paul assembled the elders of Ephesus. They were elders of this church and of no other. Throughout the Scripture, elders govern local bodies of believers—just as it was in the synagogues (Matt. 5:22; Acts 13:15; 14:23; Titus 1:5; James 5:14). What if a group of church leaders from a church down the street came to your building and declared that your church service would start an hour later than usual next week? Would you submit to their decision? Or do you not recognize clearly that such a declaration cannot have authority in your church? Those leaders cannot make the decisions for your church; only your leaders can. The same is true in every realm of authority among men.

Without membership, however, you are no more committed to the church and to her officers than a man is to a woman to whom he is not married. How can a woman submit to a husband unless she has a husband? How can a man become a husband without a vow before God that constitutes a new family? Should every man who happens to be a husband be able to call every other wife to submit to him as a husband? Unless the woman vows to submit to the man, he has no such authority over her. Likewise, in the local church, membership vows are necessary, in part, for you to fulfill the command contained in Hebrews 13:17 (to submit to your specific, local "rulers"). Membership rolls are necessary to keep record of those who have taken these vows and to know to whom the officers must keep their vows in service to God.

God's Covenantal Dealings with His People Provide a Model for Their Covenantal Dealings with the Church
God's formal constitution of His covenant with Abraham illustrates the importance of the public constitution of a covenant. In Genesis 12:1–4, God called Abraham out of Ur of the Chaldeans. This marked the beginning of a special relationship between God and Abraham's family. Abraham trusted God, and he went; God promised wonderful blessings to him. Nonetheless, in Genesis 15, God covenanted with Abraham in a formal, official manner. Although the relationship was in place already, God initiated a

formal ceremony to seal that covenant in blood. We can say at least that such a formal ceremony was not contrary to the intimate relationship that existed already between God and Abraham.

In Genesis 17, God required Abraham to covenant with Him in another official way. God required Abraham to receive and administer the covenant sign of circumcision to himself and to his descendants in order to express his covenant commitment to God and God's covenant commitment to him. By this sign, God obligated Abraham and his descendants to faith in and obedience to Him. By using and applying the sign, Abraham testified publicly his commitment to the terms of the covenant (Rom. 4:11). God did not take this sign lightly; in Genesis 17:14, the son who grew up and refused to be circumcised would be cut off from God's people.

Official covenant commitments are important in Scripture. Even the outward sign of the covenant is highly significant. This outward, official sign of commitment to God was a significant act that pointed to the substance behind the form. One might say that such formal rites were necessary only in the ceremonial worship of the Old Testament. However, the sign of baptism remains important for the church today, and we baptize all who belong to God's covenant people (Acts 2:38; 8:36; 16:34). The thief on the cross, though, was saved without baptism (Luke 23:39–43; cf. Matt. 27:44) and Simon the sorcerer was condemned in spite of baptism (Acts 8:9–24). Like circumcision before it, baptism is the public, official sign of entrance into God's covenant people. It is the sign of membership in the covenant and the church and of commitment to Christ in the context of the church. In Acts 2:41, about three thousand souls were added to the church. They were counted by means of their baptisms. These then continued in the apostles' doctrine, fellowship, breaking of bread, and prayers (Acts 2:42). In other words, officially, publicly, by baptism, they were added to Christ as those joined to His body. They became citizens of heaven through the new birth, faith in Christ, and repentance. They joined themselves to the church on earth through baptism and continued committed to its fellowship. This public, official joining with the visible church is one reason why Scripture treats baptism as so important. God covenants with us, and He gives us a sign of the covenant. We must covenant with Him through making public vows of commitment to His church.

The Discipline Process Christ Outlines in
Matthew 18:15–20 Reinforces the Need for
Formal Church Membership
Christ told His disciples that they must deal with unrepentant sin in their brethren specifically and concretely. If our brethren do not hear us after private admonition and after bringing one or two witnesses, then we must "tell it to the church." Whether you regard this as an official church court

or the membership at large, Christ assumes that the body of the church is both recognizable and definable.[5] Our Lord makes no provision in this process for dealing with churchless Christians.

However, putting someone out of the church for unrepentant sin is an exercise of the keys of the kingdom (Matt. 16:19). In fact, entrance into the church is an exercise of the keys of the kingdom just as much as exclusion from the church is. The authority symbolized by the imagery of keys is that of both opening and closing doors. While the sword, a symbol of the death penalty, represents the state's authority (Rom. 13:4); and the rod, a symbol of physical discipline, represents parental authority (Prov. 13:24; 22:15), opening and closing is the symbol of the church's authority. In Matthew 16:19, Jesus committed the keys to Peter (and spoke to Peter in the singular "you"). However, in Matthew 18:18, using the same language of "binding" and "loosing" as in Matthew 16:19, Jesus addressed the disciples in the plural ("you all"). There is now a plurality of leaders who hold the authority to bind or loose, as symbolized in the keys. This group consists of the elders of the church, which is the perpetual ruling

---

5. "The church" here likely follows Jewish use in the Old Testament and the synagogue. This referred to the eldership as the governing body that represented the church. See John Murray, "Office in the Church," in *Collected Writings of John Murray: Professor of Systematic Theology, Westminster Theological Seminary, Philadelphia, Pennsylvania, 1937–1966* (Edinburgh: Banner of Truth, 1976–), 2:357–65.

office in Christ's church. Admitting members to the church who, in light of the teaching of Scripture, make a genuine profession of faith, is a public declaration that we trust their sins are remitted graciously by means of faith in Christ and His righteousness alone. This is a positive act of church discipline that should strengthen the faith of believers. It is also a commitment. Just as you enter the church through the ministerial application of the word, so you must voluntarily place yourself under the exercise of the power of the keys. The only way to exercise discipline, both for edification and for correction, is for members to join the church through a public commitment and to be counted on her rolls.

Membership Rolls Are Essential in the Election of Church Officers

The election of church officers is both a right and a privilege of church members. In the book of Acts, the congregation participated in the election of an apostle (Acts 1:15, 21–23), the first deacons (Acts 6:3–6), and elders (Acts 14:23). Yet it is impossible to elect officers justly without a well-defined membership in the local congregation. Membership rolls are necessary in this case in order to know who has the right to vote for new officers. These membership rolls consist of those who have vowed their commitment to the local church and their submission to these elected leaders.

Without membership rolls constituted by vows, it is impossible to preserve the biblical right of church members to elect their own officers. Several problems arise, for example, when a church without membership attempts to elect a new minister. The church has two options. First, it is left at the mercy of whoever shows up on the day of the election, whether they attend the church regularly or not. In such cases it is not uncommon for attendance to double or triple on the day on which elections are held. Yet what right do those who have made no commitment to the officers and members of that congregation have to elect the future officers of the congregation? If the church has no membership, then how does anyone present have a sure right to participate in electing officers? In fact, what if the much larger church down the street decided to swarm into your building and vote for your officers? How could you prevent them from doing so, unless you recognized that only members of your particular church could vote on your officers? Second, without membership rolls, the alternative to allowing anyone present to vote is that the current leadership will bypass election by the people entirely and choose their own successors. The former option deprives church members of the right to elect those who minister regularly to them by making them subject to people who may not even attend the church regularly. The second option obliterates the New Testament example of the people electing their own officers and gives the current leadership tyrannical authority over the church. This shows that membership rolls are necessary in order to protect the rights of God's people in the local church.

OBJECTIONS TO CHURCH MEMBERSHIP

Several objections arise in relation to this topic. These include objections against the use of vows, concerns over formality in the church, or experiences of the abuse of church power.

Objection 1: Some object to the use of vows in bringing members into the church because they argue that Scripture forbids taking vows (Matt. 5:34; James 5:12). However, when Christ forbade vows He did so against those who used them as a pretense for dishonest practices (Matt. 23:16–22). By contrast, we must always let our yes be yes and our no be no. Thus, there are occasions in which the Lord commands us to take oaths in His name (Deut. 6:13; 10:20). Even God at times takes oaths in His own name in order to demonstrate the certainty of His promises to us (Gen. 22:16; Isa. 45:23; Heb. 6:13). God is the standard for our righteousness. We must imitate Him as dearly beloved children (Eph. 5:1). As a perfect man, Christ submitted to a court when it placed Him under oath (Matt. 26:63–64). Paul occasionally called upon God as his witness in order to stress the importance of his actions or teaching (e.g., Rom. 1:9; 2 Cor. 1:23). Oaths and vows are not only lawful in Scripture, but they are also necessary in some cases. We have already seen why this is the case in relation to marriage. Any relationship that carries duties, promises, and obligations with it ordinarily requires a vow to seal that relationship. It is impossible to create an official membership roll without promises on the part of members. This fits precisely the biblical description and use of vows.

Objection 2: Some may object that the early church was not as formal as ours. Church membership was not formalized as it is now. This is an argument from silence, which is always hard to prove. However, in light of passages such as Matthew 18:15–20 and Hebrews 13:17, it was necessary to have some method of keeping track of the members of the local church. In fact, according to Acts 2:41, some record of the numbers of people joining the church was kept. We must beware of determining our practice based on what we imagine the early church did or did not do. Rather, we must ask ourselves what is necessary to fulfill the teaching of Scripture regarding the church and her members. This requires formal commitment by vows and a record of members in some form.

Objection 3: What about those who have experienced the bitter abuse of authority? Just as the best Christians have wronged others at times, so even the best churches have done so. How can those who have experienced abuses of church power trust the rulers of a local church again? The simple answer to this objection is that none can assume that a church body will never abuse its authority. The scribes and Pharisees in Christ's day clearly did so. At the same time, God calls us to honor and submit to church rulers. This even included the scribes and Pharisees (Matt. 23:3). In other words, while fully acknowledging the pain that may come of it, our Lord nonetheless commands us to submit to church rulers. In a similar way, some women regret their choice of husband when a husband is not godly. If this husband violates the marriage covenant and leaves his wife for another woman, then should the woman conclude that marriage is itself a defective relationship? This would deny God's wisdom in giving marriage to bless both men and women.

We must always avoid attempting to correct an error by running to the opposite error. The fact that others abuse sex does not mandate monasticism as the best form of godly living. Paul says it is better to marry than to burn with passion (1 Cor. 7:9). Likewise, because some church officers are liable to abuse their power does not excuse us from the biblical mandate to place ourselves under and submit to church government. As in all proper relations of authority, we must submit to church government under the authority of God, to the glory of God, and in submission to God. When officers abuse their authority, then we must use the means provided in our church to confront them and, if necessary, to remove them through the processes provided by the church. The one thing that we cannot do is quit the church. Our commitment to Christ requires that we commit to His church by way of membership.

CONCLUSION

Have you become a member of a local congregation? Have you resisted having your name added to the rolls? How can you keep the commands of Christ in relation to the local church without doing so? To which elders do you actively submit? Which congregation are you committed to? You cannot adequately express your membership in the church invisible without doing so through the church visible and local. Have you resisted taking membership vows? Recognize that good vows require you to promise to do only what Scripture requires of you already. Must you not be subject to the discipline and government of the church? Should you not support the local church in its worship and work to the best of your ability? No local church is perfect, and no church need be in order for you to join it. Join the church that best reflects your understanding of Scripture, honors Christ, and feeds your soul. Take your vows freely and without coercion. Take them wisely. Take them prayerfully and seriously. But, by all means, take them.

Everything that the triune God commands you is for your good. Will His promises fail you as you seek to honor Him in His church? We should always be thankful that Christ did not call us to live the

Christian life alone. He went to the cross alone. He trod the winepress of God's wrath alone. Yet He redeemed a community of sinners. The church is His body. Belonging to her by true faith is belonging to the Father's household. She is the temple of the Holy Spirit. In spite of the faults of the church militant on earth, she is inhabited by many who hope to be part of the church triumphant in heaven. Are you citizens of this heavenly kingdom? Then reflect your membership in this heavenly society by becoming a member of the earthly society that reflects it. As William Perkins wrote, the church is "the suburbs of the city of God, and the gate of heaven; and therefore entrance must be made into heaven in and by the church."[6] Let us dwell with her and in her so that we might be near to God through her.

---

6. William Perkins, *A Warning Against the Idolatrie of the Last Times and an Instruction Touching Religious, or Divine Worship* (Cambridge: John Legat, 1601), 145.